D0558298

COMPREHENSIVE RESEARCH & STUDY GUIDES

John Steinbeck's

Of Mice and Men

Edited & with
an Introduction
by Harold Bloom

First Printing
1 3 5 7 9 8 6 4 2

The Chelsea House World Wide Web site address is
http://www.chelseahouse.com

Library of Congress Cataloging-in-Publication Data

Bloom, Harold.
John Steinbeck's Of mice and men / Harold Bloom, editor.
p. cm. — (Bloom's notes)
Includes bibliographical references and index.
Summary: Includes a brief biography of the author, thematic and structural analysis of the work, critical views, and an index of themes and ideas.
ISBN 0-7910-3668-5 (hc)   ISBN 0-7910-4143-3 (pb)
1. Steinbeck, John, 1902-1968. Of mice and men. 2. Salinas River Valley (Calif.) — in literature. 3. Friendship in literature. 4. Cowboys in literature.
[1. Steinbeck, John, 1902-1968. Of mice and men. 2. American literature — History and criticism.] I. Title. II. Series: Bloom, Harold. Bloom's notes.
PS3537.T32340418 1996
813'.52—dc20
95-34517
CIP
AC

Chelsea House Publishers
1974 Sproul Road, Suite 400
P.O. Box 914
Broomall, PA 19008-0914

Contents

Editor's Note

My Introduction centers upon the achieved aesthetic dignity of the friendship between Lennie and George, which alone saves *Of Mice and Men* from Steinbeck's heavy fatalism. For Mark Van Doren, the unrealistic nature of both characters renders the book inadequate, a judgment shared by Dorothea Brande Collins. In contrast, Joseph Wood Krutch and Harry T. Moore find Lennie and George theatrically effective, a view not shared by Maxwell Geismar.

In different ways, both Peter Lisca and Warren French emphasize the melancholy comedy of the friends' relationship, while F. W. Watt faults the book because its minor characters are insubstantial. The story of Cain and Abel is discerned beneath the surface of Steinbeck's plot by William Goldhurst, after which Howard Levant argues that the book is too simplistic to live. The play version of the story is examined by Nelson Valjean, while Sunita Jain sees Lennie as an ambivalent figure, being both victim and destroyer, Steinbeck's movement away from politics in *Of Mice and Men* is noted by Paul McCarthy, after which John H. Timmerman commends the unity of the book.

California social history of the 1930s is considered as the novel's context by Anne Loftis, while Charlotte Cook Hadella regards the book as another Steinbeckian meditation upon the American Dream.

Introduction

HAROLD BLOOM

The late Anthony Burgess, in a touching salute from one professional writer to another, commended *Of Mice and Men* as "a fine novella (or play with extended stage directions) which succeeds because it dares sentimentality." Rereading *Of Mice and Men*, I remain impressed by its economical intensity, which has authentic literary power, though the sentimentality sometimes seems to me excessive. The book has been called Darwinian and naturalistic; it does share in the kind of dramatic pathos featured also in the plays of Eugene O'Neill and the novels of Theodore Dreiser. Reality is harsh and ultimately scarcely to be borne; dreams and delusions alone allow men to keep going. George and Lennie share the hopeless dream of a little ranch of their own, where George could keep the well-meaning but disaster-prone Lennie out of trouble and sorrow. As several critics have noted, this is one of Steinbeck's recurrent dreams of a lost Eden, sadly illusory yet forever beckoning.

As in the works of O'Neill and of Dreiser, the anxiety that afflicts all of Steinbeck's male protagonists is a desperate solitude. Despite his frequent use of Biblical style, more marked in *The Grapes of Wrath* than in *Of Mice and Men*, Steinbeck was anything but a religious writer, by temperament and by belief. His heavy naturalism is very close to fatalism: Lennie is doomed by his nature, which craves affection, softness, the childlike, yet which is overwhelmingly violent and pragmatically brutal because of childish bafflement and defensiveness. What could anyone have done to save Lennie? Since George is truly responsible and caring and still fails to keep Lennie safe, it seems clear that even institutionalization could not have saved Steinbeck's most pathetic version of natural man. That returns the burden of Steinbeck's sad fable to Steinbeck himself: What has the author done for himself as a novelist by telling us this overdetermined story, and what do we gain as readers by attending to it? Though there are dramatic values in *Of Mice and Men*, they are inadequate compared to O'Neill at his best. There is an authentic dignity in the brotherhood of George and

Lennie, but it too seems stunted compared to the massive humanity of the major figures in Dreiser's strongest narratives, *Sister Carrie* and *An American Tragedy*. Clearly there is something that endures in *Of Mice and Men* as in *The Grapes of Wrath*, though the novella lacks the social force of Steinbeck's major novel. Is it the stoic minimalism of George and Lennie and their fellow wandering ranch hands that somehow achieves a memorable image of human value?

Steinbeck resented Hemingway because he owed Hemingway too much, both in style and in the perception of the aesthetic dignity of natural men, at once unable to bear either society or solitude. The counterinfluence in *Of Mice and Men* seems to be the Faulkner of *The Sound and the Fury*, particularly in the representation of poor Lennie, who may have in him a trace of the benign idiot, Benjy. Any comparison of Faulkner and Steinbeck will tend to lessen Steinbeck, who is overmatched by Faulkner's mythic inventiveness and consistent strength of characterization. Yet there is a mythic quality to *Of Mice and Men*, a clear sense that Lennie and George ultimately represent something larger than either their selves or their relationship. They touch a permanence because their mutual care enhances both of them. That care cannot save Lennie, and it forces George to execute his friend to save him from the hideous violence of a mob. But the care survives Lennie's death; Slim's recognition of the dignity and the value of the care is the novel's final gesture, and is richly shared by the reader. ❖

Biography of John Steinbeck

John Ernst Steinbeck, Jr., was born on February 27, 1902, to John Ernst and Olive Hamilton Steinbeck in Salinas, a small agricultural community in the north central part of California. He read voraciously as a youth; he was particularly fascinated by Sir Thomas Malory's *Morte d'Arthur* (c. 1470), and this retelling of the legends of King Arthur influenced him for his whole life. Steinbeck graduated from Salinas High School in 1919 and entered Stanford University the next year, taking courses in science and becoming interested in marine biology. Although he studied at Stanford intermittently for five years, he finally left without a degree.

In 1925 Steinbeck moved to New York City, where he began working for a newspaper, the New York *American.* He was a very poor reporter, however, because he would get too emotionally involved in the stories he was writing, so he returned to California by working as a deckhand on a ship. Finding a job as a caretaker in Lake Tahoe, Nevada, he devoted himself to writing and produced an adventure story about a Caribbean pirate, *Cup of Gold,* published in 1929. The next year he married Carol Henning and settled in Pacific Grove, California. At this time he formed a close friendship with noted marine biologist Edward F. Ricketts, who for many years was Steinbeck's mentor and critic. Their expedition in 1940 to the Gulf of California was the basis for *Sea of Cortez* (1941), and Ricketts appears as a character in several other works.

Steinbeck's first book went largely unnoticed, as did his next two, *The Pastures of Heaven* (1932) and *To a God Unknown* (1933), both of which are set in California. His first significant recognition came with the publication of *Tortilla Flat* (1935), a tale of Mexican-American vagabonds in the Monterey area. The $3,000 Steinbeck received for the movie rights to this short novel helped to lift him out of the poverty he had experienced as a struggling writer in the Great Depression. In 1936 his novel *In Dubious Battle,* dealing with a fruit pickers' strike in California, caused considerable controversy. The next year

Steinbeck cemented his reputation with *Of Mice and Men* (1937), which remains one of the most widely read works in American literature. Steinbeck was praised for his accomplishments as a writer in the American idiom, and the play version of *Of Mice and Men* (1937), on which he worked with the famous playwright George S. Kaufman, won the New York Drama Critics' Circle Award and was made into a film starring Burgess Meredith and Lon Chaney, Jr. Steinbeck used the proceeds from the book and play to travel widely in Europe.

Returning to California, Steinbeck spent much time in the camps of migrant workers. This led directly to *The Grapes of Wrath* (1939), an epic of dispossessed Oklahoma sharecroppers in search of a promised land in California. The novel was extremely topical and also crystallized themes that remained prominent in Steinbeck's writings thereafter: concern for the working classes, the preying of men upon one another, and sentimental attachments to land and community. It was the best-selling book of 1939, won the Pulitzer Prize for fiction in 1940, and was made into an acclaimed film.

Steinbeck divorced his wife, Carol, in 1942 and married Gwyndolen Conger the next year; they had two sons. Much of his writing of this period focused on World War II, including *Bombs Away* (1942), a book designed to convince Americans of the importance of the air force, and *The Moon Is Down* (1942), a short novel about the German occupation of a small town in Norway. He spent the latter half of 1943 in Europe as a special correspondent for the *New York Herald Tribune,* and his reports were later collected as *Once There Was a War* (1958). Steinbeck was traumatized by the suffering he witnessed among the troops; as if to banish these memories, upon his return he wrote the novel *Cannery Row* (1945), a nostalgic look at life in Monterey before the war.

In 1945 Steinbeck settled in New York City with his wife and sons. In 1947 he published the well-known short novel *The Pearl,* an allegory based on a Mexican folk tale. A trip to Russia in 1947 led to the writing of *A Russian Journal* (1948), with photographs by Robert Capa. Although Steinbeck was elected to the American Academy of Arts and Letters, both his personal life and his literary career became troubled around this time: he divorced his wife in 1948; his friend Ed Ricketts died in an accident; and his recent works were poorly received, especially the play *Burning Bright* (1950), which closed after only thirteen performances on Broadway. Steinbeck turned to writing screenplays, including the radical political film *Viva Zapata!* (1950), directed by Elia Kazan. In 1950 he married Elaine Scott.

While living alternately in New York and Nantucket, Steinbeck wrote *East of Eden* (1952), a long novel about a man who marries a prostitute; it partly restored his literary reputation. He and his wife spent the next several years in Europe, and Steinbeck sent reports of his travels to *Collier's* and the *Saturday Review*. He returned to the United States briefly in 1952 to work as a speechwriter for Adlai Stevenson's presidential campaign.

Steinbeck settled in Sag Harbor, Long Island, in 1955, and the next year he again assisted in Adlai Stevenson's bid for the presidency; but after Stevenson lost, Steinbeck spent much of the next three years in England studying Malory's *Morte d'Arthur*. The light-hearted political satire *The Short Reign of Pippin IV* was published in 1957. Steinbeck's final novel was *The Winter of Our Discontent* (1961), a story of life in Long Island.

Disillusioned by the failure of Adlai Stevenson's third presidential bid in 1960 (he lost the Democratic nomination to John F. Kennedy), Steinbeck set out to rediscover America, in the company of his dog Charley. The three-month trip in the latter half of 1960 led to the writing of *Travels with Charley* (1962), a work that did much to restore Steinbeck's fading reputation. In 1962 he was also awarded the Nobel Prize for literature. Steinbeck continued to spend much time traveling in Europe, although he returned to the United States in 1964 to work on Lyndon B. Johnson's presidential campaign. At this time he also received the United States Medal of Freedom. In 1965 he began writing a series of letters to Alicia Paterson Guggenheim, publisher of the Long Island newspaper *Newsday,* from various locations around the world, including Israel and Vietnam. These letters were controversial for their criticism of the increasing rebelliousness of American youth and for their support of

American involvement in the Vietnam War. A later volume, *America and Americans* (1966), repeats some of these criticisms but otherwise affirms Steinbeck's faith in his country's future.

John Steinbeck died in New York City on December 20, 1968. Many of his letters and uncollected essays have been published posthumously, but Steinbeck's reputation continues to rest on his searing political and social novels of the 1930s. Although scorned by some critics for being superficial and excessively moralistic, he remains one of the most popular and respected American authors of the century. ✤

Thematic and Structural Analysis

Ranked by some critics among John Steinbeck's greatest works, *Of Mice and Men*, published in 1937, is the story of two migrant farm workers and their elusive dreams of possessing their own land. The novel depicts a series of powerless characters, all of whom must struggle to maintain their humanity and cultivate their dreams in the face of overwhelming forces of dehumanization. Though it is set in California during the Great Depression, *Of Mice and Men* transcends the particulars of time and place in its theme of the hopes and aspirations of the dispossessed. Written between Steinbeck's two powerful novels of agrarian conflict, *In Dubious Battle* and his most famous work, *The Grapes of Wrath*, this "play/novelette," as the author called it, is exceptional for its experimentation with form. Though it is familiar to most readers as a novel, Steinbeck intended *Of Mice and Men* to be easily transferable to the stage. The division of the work into six sections, or "scenes," in which lighting elements evoke a sense of the stage, and the meticulous "set" descriptions at the beginning of each section are both techniques of stage writing incorporated into the novel form. Moreover, Steinbeck relies heavily on dialogue rather than on traditional narrative to present his characters, and their entrances and exits are carefully described.

Section one opens, as does each of the novel's parts, with a description of the setting, in this case the idyllic California countryside, where "the Salinas River drops in close to the hillside bank and runs deep and green." Though the description is of an isolated spot, where lizards, rabbits, and deer come for water, the path that runs through the trees has been "beaten hard by boys coming down from the ranches to swim in the deep pool, and beaten hard by tramps who come wearily down from the highway." This is a landscape frequently traveled, and the story about to unfold is meant to be universal.

Into this place of rest and quiet enter Lennie and George, weary from a day of foot travel on the hot state highway.

Though dressed similarly in denim, with "black, shapeless hats," physically the two men could not be more different. George is described as "small and quick, dark of face, with restless eyes and sharp, strong features," while Lennie appears to be more animal than man, "with wide, sloping shoulders . . . dragging his feet a little, the way a bear drags his paws." Lennie's animalism—throughout the novel he may be said to represent the animal nature of humankind—is emphasized by his thirsty rush for the water. He drinks "with long gulps, snorting into the water like a horse," while George drinks carefully from his hand in quick scoops. Lennie's doglike devotion to George quickly becomes apparent as he imitates the other man's every move, even down to adjusting the tilt of his hat.

After they drink, George speaks aloud, addressing himself as much as his companion. He complains about the "bastard bus driver" who informed them incorrectly about the distance to their destination. During a break in his tirade Lennie timidly asks, "Where we goin', George?" George's response, initially expressing irritation but finally patience and kindness, is characteristic of the way he handles Lennie's often-redundant questions throughout the novel. As George recounts their steps over the past few days, it becomes apparent that Lennie is entirely unable to think for himself and must have the simplest details of his day recounted for him by George. George notices that Lennie has been hiding something in his coat pocket and insists that Lennie hand it over. "Jus' a dead mouse, George. I didn' kill it. Honest! I found it. I found it dead," Lennie protests. He relinquishes the mouse, which George promptly throws to the other side of the pool.

When their conversation resumes, George tells Lennie that they are headed south to work on a ranch, and several times he tells Lennie he must not speak when they meet their new boss, lest the boss think Lennie is crazy and refuse to hire them. George also admonishes Lennie not to do any of the bad things he did in Weed, where the two men were run out of town. Recalling this earlier trouble reminds George of the difficulty of caring for Lennie, and he muses on how simple his life would be without him. "I could live so easy and maybe have a girl," he says to himself.

During preparations for their supper, Lennie surreptitiously retrieves the dead mouse from the far side of the pool and once again has to relinquish it. George tells him, "I ain't takin' it away jus' for meanness. That mouse ain't fresh, Lennie; and besides, you've broke it pettin' it." Lennie apparently has a history of "breaking" mice, as George reminds him. For the second time, Lennie brings up the matter of rabbits: "I wish't we'd get the rabbits pretty soon, George. They ain't so little."

As they eat their supper of canned beans, Lennie remarks that he wishes he had ketchup, provoking a long outburst from George about the inconvenience Lennie causes him and the painless life he could have on his own. The reader learns at this point that Lennie's crime in Weed was "feeling" a girl's dress. At the end of his tirade, however, George looks "across the fire at Lennie's anguished face, and then he [looks] ashamedly at the flames." Clearly, whatever hardship caring for Lennie entails, George is attached to his companion and regrets his occasional bursts of temper and impatience.

As a gesture of reconciliation, George promises Lennie a puppy. Sensing George's change of mood, Lennie asks George to tell him "The Story," which he asks George to repeat throughout the novel. George's speech about the farm they hope to own—a speech that Lennie interrupts periodically with his own well-rehearsed additions—is their declaration of self-worth and the articulation of their shared dream of economic stability and companionship. "Guys like us, that work on ranches," George begins, "are the loneliest guys in the world. They got no family. They don't belong no place." Lennie excitedly urges George to "tell how it is," and he obliges: "With us it ain't like that," George says. "We got a future. We got somebody to talk to that gives a damn about us." He continues:

> "Someday—we're gonna get the jack together and we're gonna have a little house and a couple of acres an' a cow and some pigs and—"
>
> "*An' live off the fatta the lan',*" Lennie shouted. "*An' have rabbits.*"

Section one closes with Lennie promising to return to this spot, hide in the brush, and wait for George if he gets into trouble. The final image is of a peacefully dimming fire and whispering breeze.

The bunkhouse where George and Lennie make their appearance the next day (**section two**) is a simple rectangular building, sparsely furnished with bunks for eight men, small shelves for their personal possessions, a single cast-iron stove, and a common table where the men play cards. In the style of a drama, Steinbeck sets the stage by describing the bunkhouse before the two friends enter, accompanied by "a tall, stoop-shouldered old man," Candy, a "swamper" or handyman. In response to George's questioning, Candy describes the boss as generally decent, and tells how he gave a gallon of whisky to the ranch hands as a Christmas gift.

The boss, when he does appear, is described primarily in terms of his clothing, which marks him as a man of relative importance and power. "He wore blue jean trousers, a flannel shirt, a black, unbuttoned vest and a black coat. His thumbs were stuck in his belt, on each side of a square steel buckle . . . he wore high-heeled boots and spurs to prove he was not a laboring man." George introduces himself and Lennie and explains their lateness as the fault of the bus driver, speaking all the while for Lennie. At one point, forgetting George's instructions to remain silent, Lennie echoes George's description of him as "strong as a bull." George's fierce scowl reminds Lennie not to speak again. Once he recognizes Lennie's mental deficiencies, the boss questions George's motivation and remarks, "I never seen one guy take so much trouble for another guy." To the boss, Lennie is not so much a human being as an economic resource, something to be sold. George protests that Lennie is his cousin and was "kicked in the head by a horse when he was a kid." Momentarily placated but still suspicious, the boss leaves the bunkhouse after assigning the men to Slim's team. After he leaves, George turns on Lennie for answering the boss himself: "Now he's got his eye on us. Now we got to be careful and not make no slips." He even accuses Candy, who reenters the bunkhouse, of "listenin' " from outside the open front door.

Candy is accompanied by his "dragfooted sheep dog, gray of muzzle, and with pale, blind old eyes." He is followed shortly by Curley, a small young man with curly hair who, like his father the boss, is wearing high-heeled boots. Curley immediately strikes a belligerent pose before George and Lennie, directing most of his aggression at Lennie. After Curley leaves, the swamper explains that Curley is "handy"—he is a boxer, and he "hates big guys. He's alla time picking scraps with big guys. Kind of like he's mad at 'em because he ain't a big guy." Since his marriage, Candy continues, Curley seems "cockier'n ever," perhaps because his wife has "got the eye," often flirting with the ranch hands.

When Candy leaves, George repeatedly warns Lennie to stay clear of Curley and tries to make Lennie remember where they are to meet if Lennie gets in trouble. Their conversation is interrupted by the appearance of Curley's wife, who is ostensibly looking for her husband. Though pretty, she is heavily made up, and her voice possesses "a nasal, brittle quality." She lingers in the bunkhouse doorway, flirting with the men, but leaves quickly when she realizes that Curley may be looking for her at the main house. Lennie is fascinated by the woman, repeatedly murmuring, "she's purty." Enraged, George tells Lennie, "Don't you even take a look at that bitch. I don't care what she says and what she does. I seen 'em poison before, but I never seen no piece of jail bait worse than her. You leave her be." George's fierce reaction frightens Lennie, who says, "I don' like this place, George. This ain't no good place. I wanna get outta here." George, while agreeing with Lennie, knows they must stay to make their money. He promises they will leave as soon as possible.

As the clatter of men washing reaches the bunkhouse, Slim enters. Slim is the unquestioned "prince of the ranch," admired for his consummate skill as a "jerkline skinner" (mule driver) and for his solid character and dignified bearing. Kind, intelligent, and fair, he is clearly in a class apart from the other characters George and Lennie encounter. He is the first person on the ranch to speak neither with hostility nor with suspicion to Lennie and George, and in contrast to the boss's suspicious appraisal of George's relationship with Lennie, Slim immediately appreciates the advantages of a partnership. "Ain't many guys travel around together," he muses. "I don't know why. Maybe ever'body in the whole damn world is scared of each other."

Their friendly chatter is joined by Carlson, a "barley bucker," one of the farmhands who load harvested bales of grain after threshing. Slim's dog Lulu has just given birth to a litter of pups, so Carlson suggests that Slim "get Candy to shoot his old dog and give him one of the pups to raise up," since Candy's old dog is smelly and nearly unable to walk. During this exchange, George stares "intently" at Slim, awaiting his reaction to Carlson's practical but brutal suggestion. He knows how attached Candy is to his old dog. As soon as the other men leave, Lennie excitedly brings up the subject of getting one of the pups. As George and Lennie are leaving for dinner, Curley storms in looking for his wife, then leaves as abruptly as he came. Candy's old dog returns to the empty bunkhouse and sinks quietly to the floor.

By the close of section two, the reader has been introduced to all the novel's main characters. The petty cruelty and smallness of Curley contrasts with the calm dignity and kindness of Slim; Candy and George, both powerless, gentle men, are each paired with a beloved but burdensome companion.

At the end of the workday, Slim and George enter the darkened bunkhouse together to open **section three**. We learn that Slim has agreed to give a pup to Lennie, and the two men discuss Lennie's physical strength and his simplemindedness. In the warmth of sudden friendship, George tells Slim that he and Lennie grew up in the same town and that he began caring for Lennie after the death of Lennie's aunt Clara. The two men agree that Lennie "ain't a bit mean." But, George tells Slim, Lennie always finds trouble because of his feeble intellect. Eventually George confides that Lennie was accused of raping a girl in Weed after he had "petted" her dress and held on in panic when she screamed. The men had to flee when a lynch party was organized against Lennie.

Moments later Lennie comes in, concealing his new pup under his coat. George reprimands him for taking such a young pup from its mother and tells him to take it back to the barn. Slim comments that Lennie is "jes' like a kid."

The men are soon joined by Candy and Carlson, who begins to complain about the stink of Candy's dog, asking Candy why he does not shoot the animal. Candy protests that he has had the dog "since he was a pup," but Carlson persists, offering to shoot the dog himself. Slim offers Candy one of his pups and, in a decisive moment, agrees with Carlson that the old dog should be killed. Though Candy continues to protest weakly, Slim's decision is law in the bunkhouse, and the swamper soon gives in. Carlson takes out his pistol and leads the dog out of the bunkhouse, agreeing, at Slim's reminder, to bury the corpse.

The men try to make small talk while they listen for the shot. George nervously shuffles cards at the common table. Finally, they hear a distant shot and look quickly at the old man, who turns his face to the wall in silence.

Crooks, the black stable buck, comes in to tell Slim he has warmed some tar for a mule's foot, and Slim leaves to apply it. Whit, another ranch hand, and George discuss Curley's wife and the trouble she can cause; the men chat about the two brothels in town. Lennie and Carlson return together, and Carlson begins cleaning his gun, without looking at Candy. Lennie slinks to his bunk. Suddenly, Curley bursts into the room, looking for his wife and Slim. He heads for the barn in search of them, followed by Whit and Carlson, who hope for a fight.

Lennie and George talk quietly about the pups. "Slim says I better not pet them pups so much for a while," Lennie tells George, and George questions his friend about Curley's wife and Slim. Had he seen them in the barn together? What was Slim doing? Satisfied that there will not be trouble, George begins to play solitaire and reminds Lennie to stay away from that "tart." Lennie asks, "George, how long's it gonna be till we get that little place an' live on the fatta the lan'—an' rabbits?" Candy listens quietly from his bunk as George once again tells The Story to Lennie, this time describing the kinds of food they will grow, their snug little house with its extra bunk for friends, and the pleasures of working their own land for their own benefit. He promises Lennie he can feed and care for his own rabbits by bringing them alfalfa in their cages.

Candy jumps up from his bunk, asking George if he really knows of such a place. George says he does, that the owners of the house are broke and looking to sell. Candy offers to throw in his savings—"three hunderd an' fifty bucks"—if they will let him join in with them. Suddenly, the men realize the possibility of their dream: "They fell into a silence. They looked at one another, amazed. . . . 'Jesus Christ! I bet we could swing her,' " George says aloud. He begins to think about the advantages of having their own place, how they could come and go whenever they pleased, even taking a day off work for a carnival or circus. When Lennie asks, "When we gon'ta do it, George?" he replies, "In one month. Right squack in one month. . . . I'm gon'ta write to them old people that owns the place that we'll take it." Hearing voices outside, George warns his companions not to tell anyone about their plans. Before the other men enter, Candy turns to George and says, "I ought to of shot that dog myself, George. I shouldn't ought to of let no stranger shoot my dog."

Slim, Curley, Carlson, and Whit enter the bunkhouse, Curley apologizing to Slim for nagging him about his wife. Carlson and Candy begin to tease Curley for his cowardice before Slim. In embarrassment and anger, Curley looks around the room for a way to vent his rage, and his eyes light on Lennie, "still smiling with delight at the memory of the ranch." Thinking Lennie is laughing at him, Curley attacks Lennie, who cries for George's help but does nothing to defend himself. After Curley punches George several times, Slim jumps up to intervene but is stopped by George, who yells out, "Get 'im, Lennie!" Lennie reaches out and stops Curley's fist midswing, enveloping it in his huge "paw." Curley begins "flopping like a fish on a line" and is soon reduced to helpless crying. George slaps Lennie repeatedly to get him to release his hold, but Curley's hand has been crushed, and the other men prepare to take him to a doctor in Soledad. Before they leave, Slim tells Curley, "I think you got your han' caught in a machine," warning him that if he tries to have George and Lennie fired, they will tell what really happened, "an' then will [he] get the laugh." Curley agrees to keep silent. After the men leave, Lennie worries that George will not let him tend his rabbits because of the fight. George reassures him and sends him out to wash his face.

Section four opens in a new setting, the harness room where Crooks, the black stable buck, has his bunk and possessions, including a few books, a shotgun, and several pairs of shoes. Crooks is described as a "proud, aloof man," bent over in pain by his crooked spine, which he rubs with liniment.

Lennie quietly appears in the doorway, smiling in an attempt to make friends, and despite Crooks' initial resistance Lennie's guilelessness and offer of company finally win him over. Lennie begins chattering about the "little place" they are going to get and the rabbits he will soon have in his care, and Crooks thinks the big man is crazy. He begins telling Lennie about his life, about the isolation of being the only black man for miles around. He observes, "George can tell you screwy things, and it don't matter. It's just the talking. It's just bein' with another guy. That's all."

Crooks asks Lennie what he would do if George never returned from town, where he and the other men have gone to visit a brothel: "[J]us' s'pose he don't come back. What'll you do then? . . . They'll take ya to the booby hatch. They'll tie ya up with a collar, like a dog." Fearful and angry, Lennie approaches Crooks menacingly, asking, "Who hurt George?" Sensing Lennie's growing agitation (and potential violence), Crooks retreats, explaining that his own loneliness has made him a bit crazy, that a man needs another man around to confirm his sense of reality.

When Candy comes by looking for Lennie, Crooks invites him in, trying to "conceal his pleasure with anger." As Crooks begins to reminisce dreamily about his own childhood, Lennie joins in with his vision of the farm and of his rabbits. Crooks scoffs at the dream, saying every man who passes through the ranch has the same story. But Candy reinforces Lennie's story and tells Crooks about the farm and how soon they will own it. When Crooks realizes that Candy is speaking in earnest, he hesitantly offers to join in with them, saying he will work for nothing if they will let him live on their farm.

Their vision is disrupted suddenly by the appearance of Curley's wife, who asks whether any of the men have seen Curley, even though she knows he is at the brothel with the rest of the ranch hands. "They left all the weak ones here," she observes. Crooks and Candy ask her to leave, saying they do not want any trouble, but she refuses. She speaks of her dissatisfaction with Curley, her dreams of becoming an actress, and her need for company on this Saturday night, even if the only company she can find is "a nigger an' a dum-dum and a lousy ol' sheep." Candy indignantly tells her that she is not wanted in their midst, and that if she has them fired they have their own land and their own friends to turn to. She responds with disdain and, noticing the bruises on Lennie's face, begins teasing him flirtatiously, asking him where they came from. Confused and embarrassed, Lennie replies, "He got his han' caught in a machine," and she laughs, "O.K., Machine. I'll talk to you later. I like machines."

Finally Crooks tries to throw her out of his room and threatens to talk to the boss about her. She fires back, "Listen, Nigger . . . You know what I can do to you if you open your trap?" The implication, of course, is that she can have him lynched, and Crooks abjectly retreats. Curley's wife, like all characters in the novel with any power, attacks only the weak and vulnerable. When she finally leaves, the men try to bolster one another's wounded pride, but the damage is done. Crooks asks Candy to forget his offer to live on their farm in exchange for work. The dream of his own place has been shattered by Curley's wife, who has reminded him of his "place." Candy and Lennie leave with George, who has returned from town, and the scene closes with Crooks again rubbing liniment on his sore back.

At the opening of **section five**, Lennie sits quietly in the peaceful barn while the other men are heard outside playing horseshoes. Before him lies the body of a dead puppy, which he strokes from time to time. Lennie worries aloud that since his puppy "got killed," George will not let him tend his rabbits. His mood swings from remorse to anger and fear; he is first burying the puppy in the hay and then hurling it from him.

While Lennie sits absorbed in his own sorrow, Curley's wife appears, dressed and made up in her usual fashion. Though Lennie tries to avoid conversation, she says she is lonely and wants only to talk. She tries to console Lennie over the loss of the pup, saying he can easily get another. As they talk, she begins revealing herself to Lennie, her words pouring out "in a passion of communication, as though she hurried before her listener could be taken away." Moving closer, she tells Lennie about her lost chance to become a movie star, and Lennie moves still closer to her to tell her how he loves the feel of rabbits and other soft things, and how now that he has killed the puppy, "George ain't gonna let me tend no rabbits." She offers to let Lennie stroke her hair, but as he pets more and more forcefully, she begins to panic and cry, which in turn causes Lennie to panic. He covers her mouth and nose in an attempt to silence her, crying with fright and begging her to be silent so George will not hear. When she tries to break free, he shakes her more and more violently, finally breaking her neck.

Realizing that he has "done a bad thing," Lennie first tries to cover the woman with hay as he did with the dog, then grabs his dead puppy and heads for the brush, where George told him to go if he got into trouble. Once Lennie is gone, the author leaves the reader in the barn with the fading light and the half-hidden body of Curley's wife, as the sounds of the men outside grow faint. A pigeon flies through the door and flies out again. A dog enters, detects the scent of a dead body, and rushes away to her puppies. The scene is one of utter stillness: "[A] moment settled and hovered and remained for much more than a moment. And sound stopped and movement stopped for much, much more than a moment."

Then the sound of horses and halter chains and men playing horseshoes resumes, and Candy's voice calls for Lennie. When Candy discovers the body of Curley's wife, he runs for George, as the barn sounds grow louder and more insistent.

Knowing immediately who killed her, George tries to reassure himself, thinking aloud, "Maybe they'll lock 'im up an' be nice to 'im," but Candy knows better and tells George that Curley will organize a lynch party. "I ain't gonna let 'em hurt Lennie," George tells Candy. At the same moment George and Candy realize that their almost-concrete dream of owning a farm has been shattered. George asks Candy to bring in the other men but to pretend not to have told him. With George gone, Candy lashes out at Curley's wife for destroying their dream, repeating fragments of The Story. Then he leaves the barn weeping.

The men crowd quickly into the barn, and Curley vows to "kill the big son-of-a-bitch myself. I'll shoot 'im in the guts." After Curley leaves, George tells Slim that Lennie probably headed south; he asks Slim if they could bring him in and lock him up, but Slim tells George, "Curley's gonna want to shoot 'im. . . . An' s'pose they lock him up an' strap him down and put him in a cage. That ain't no good, George." Carlson bursts into the barn with Curley and, having discovered his gun is missing, claims that Lennie has stolen it. The news further infuriates Curley, and despite the efforts of George and Slim to dissuade him, he vows once again to kill Lennie. The men head out in search of Lennie, leaving Candy alone in the barn with the body.

Lennie has indeed gone back to the brush to await George, and it is here that **section six** begins, with a description of the same scene that opened the novel. Lennie appears, kneels by the pool, and drinks, "barely touching his lips to the water," as an animal would drink. As he sits by the water's edge, he imagines Aunt Clara before him, berating him for getting in trouble and causing problems for George. Then he sees a giant rabbit, which taunts him, telling him that George will beat him and abandon him. Suddenly George appears from the brush and sits quietly down by Lennie. At Lennie's urging, he repeats in monotone his usual words of recrimination and finishes by reassuring Lennie, as he always has, that he wants Lennie to stay with him.

Lennie then asks George to "[t]ell [him] like [he] done before" about how they are family to one another. In joyous tones, Lennie finishes George's speech: "We got each other, that's what."

As the breeze picks up and the sound of approaching men grows louder, George tells Lennie to take off his hat. Again, he repeats The Story for Lennie while he quietly takes Carlson's gun out of his pocket. After describing their farm and Lennie's rabbits, George tells him, "Ever'body gonna be nice to you. Ain't gonna be no more trouble. Nobody gonna hurt nobody nor steal from 'em," expanding their private farm to a universal vision of peace and kindness. It is a spoiled vision, however, as both the reader and George now know. Lennie begs, "Le's get that place now," and George replies, "Sure, right now," as he puts the gun to the back of Lennie's head and pulls the trigger.

The other men, drawn by the sound of the shot, hurry to the riverside. Slim alone understands that George has killed his friend in an act of mercy, and tries to comfort him. In response to Carlson's questions, George lies and says that he took the gun from Lennie before shooting him. Slim helps George to his feet, saying, "You hadda, George. I swear you hadda." He leads George away to get a drink while Curley and Carlson look on uncomprehendingly. Carlson says, "Now what the hell ya suppose is eatin' them two guys?"

Though the scope of Steinbeck's "play/novelette" is narrow, the implications are universal. The author's delineation of his disaffected characters, with their individual aspirations and their unique brands of loneliness, stands in stark contrast to the broader themes of friendship and shared dreams, powerlessness and loss. Steinbeck's use of stage elements—his tightly circumscribed scenes, the careful lighting, his method of "stopping" the action of the plot with silence—heightens the characters' sense of frustration and entrapment and emphasizes the constraints, both personal and societal, under which they are forced to live. Although specific conflicts ultimately lead to their destruction, the blame lies with no character in particular, but in the unpredictability of life itself. ❖

—Ann M. Brunjes
New York University

List of Characters

Lennie Small is a huge, gentle, well-meaning mentally handicapped man who is completely dependent on his friend George for protection and guidance. His prodigious strength, combined with his simple mind and his pleasure in petting soft things, leads inevitably to tragedy. Lennie may be said to represent humanity at its most basic and animalistic, and the other characters respond to him as they might to pets or farm animals, either with violence or with affection and kindness.

George Milton, Lennie's protector, companion, and friend, is an economically disenfranchised migrant worker who dreams of owning land while doubting the possibility of ever seeing that dream fulfilled. George has a complex relationship with Lennie, by turns frustrated and angry, loving and warm. When he shoots Lennie at the campsite, he acts mercifully in response to the violent, brutal world in which both men have struggled to survive. *plus his like / great pleasure*

Slim, the insightful and empathetic mule driver, is the "prince of the ranch," admired and respected by all. After Lennie crushes Curley's hand, Slim warns the boss's son not to have Lennie and George fired—and Curley heeds his warning. Slim is the only character who appreciates the depth of George's relationship with Lennie, and he alone understands why George ultimately kills his friend.

Candy, the "swamper" or handyman, is an old ranch hand kept on by the owners because he lost his hand in a farm accident. His offer of his savings and his promise to will his remaining fortune to George and Lennie persuade George to include him in their plans to buy a farm. Candy's relationship with his old dog, which is shot by another ranch hand, parallels George's relationship with Lennie.

Curley, the boss's pugnacious son, is a lightweight boxer who, insecure in his small stature and possessive of his pretty wife, constantly looks for a fight. His unprovoked attack on Lennie leads to his comeuppance: The big man crushes his hand and leaves him crying helplessly.

Curley's wife, lonely and dissatisfied, dreams of becoming a Hollywood actress. Nameless throughout the novel, she is identified only in reference to Curley, implying her status as mere property. Her only source of power is her beauty, and she incessantly flirts with—and sometimes taunts—the even more powerless ranch hands. Though she causes Lennie's destruction, she is not an entirely unsympathetic character, for as a woman in this setting she is as much a victim as George and Lennie are victims of a brutal economic system.

Carlson, a ranch hand, shoots Candy's dog after pressuring Candy to "put the old devil out of his misery." When George kills Lennie in the final scene, he uses Carlson's stolen gun— the same one used to shoot the dog—and this element reinforces the parallel between the scenes.

Crooks, the black stable buck, longs for companionship but is isolated from the other ranch hands by his race. His brief dream of joining Lennie, George, and Candy on their farm is shattered when Curley's wife brutally reminds him of what happens to black men when they "forget their place." ❖

Critical Views

MARK VAN DOREN ON THE UNREALISTIC CHARACTERS IN *OF MICE AND MEN*

[Mark Van Doren (1894–1972), the younger brother of
Carl Van Doren, was an American critic, poet, and novelist. His *Collected Poems* (1939) won a Pulitzer Prize.
Among his critical works are *Henry David Thoreau*
(1916), *The Poetry of John Dryden* (1931), and
Nathaniel Hawthorne (1949). In this review, Van Doren
criticizes *Of Mice and Men* for its unrealistic central
characters, who are either too far above or below the
norm of humanity.]

All but one of the persons in Mr. Steinbeck's extremely brief
novel are subhuman if the range of the word human is under-
stood to coincide with the range thus far established by fiction.
Two of them are evil, one of them is dangerous without meaning to be, and all of them are ignorant—all of them, that is,
except the one who shall be named hereafter. Far from knowing the grammar of conduct, they do not even know its orthog-
raphy. No two of their thoughts are consecutive, nor for that
matter do they think; it is rather that each of them follows
some instinct as a bull follows the chain which runs through a
hole in his nose, or as a crab moves toward its prey. The scene
is a ranch in California, and the bunk-house talk is terrific—God
damn, Jesus Christ, what the hell, you crazy bastard, I gotta gut
ache, and things like that. The dialect never varies, just as the
story never runs uphill.

George and Lennie, the itinerant workers who come to the
ranch one day with a dream of the little farm they will own as
soon as they get the jack together, seem to think their new job
will last at least that long; but the reader knows from the
beginning that it will not last, for Lennie is a half-witted giant
with a passion for petting mice—or rabbits, or pups, or girls—
and for killing them when they don't like it. He is doomed in
this book to kill Curley's wife; that is obvious; and then—.
Lennie, you see, cannot help shaking small helpless creatures
until their necks are broken, just as George cannot relinquish

his dream, and just as Curley cannot ever stop being a beast of jealousy. They are wound up to act that way, and the best they can do is run down; which is what happens when Mr. Steinbeck comes to his last mechanical page. ⟨. . .⟩

Mr. Steinbeck, I take it, has not been interested in reality of any kind. His jerkline skinner (mule driver) is as hopelessly above the human range as Lennie or Candy or Curley's painted wife is below it. All is extreme here; everybody is a doll; and if there is a kick in the story it is given us from some source which we cannot see, as when a goose walks over our grave, or as when in the middle of the night, the telephone rings sharply and it is the wrong number. We shall remember it about that long.

—Mark Van Doren, "Wrong Number," *Nation*, 10 March 1937, p. 275

❖

DOROTHEA BRANDE COLLINS ON THE SENTIMENTALITY OF *OF MICE AND MEN*

[Dorothea Brande Collins was a literary critic and reviewer. In this review, Collins argues that Steinbeck's short novel is excessively sentimental and its characters wooden and stereotyped.]

As for *Of Mice and Men*—surely no more sentimental wallowing ever passed for a novel, or had such a welcome, as this sad tale of a huge half-wit and his cowboy protector! Mr. Steinbeck this time wrings the Tears of Things from a ten-gallon hat, and reviewers who cannot bear the mawkishness of a Milne, the crudity of a Coward, or the mysticism of a Morgan were able to take the sorrowful symmetries of a Steinbeck to their hearts and write their reviews with tears running down their cheeks.

Who does not know by this time of Lennie, who loved to stroke soft furry things, but didn't know his own strength? Of Slim, with the "God-like eyes", knight *sans peur et sans reproche* of the bunkhouse? Of George, who loved Lennie well enough to shoot him? Of "Curley's wife", that wax-dummy girl who might have come straight out of the window of a chain dress-shop, so glossy, so hard, so brightly painted—and so far from ever having drawn a breath?

Mr. Steinbeck is "economical." He is, indeed. That is perhaps the secret of his charm. I feel sure that all those reviewers who cheered so hard for *Of Mice and Men* would, if they could have been caught while still sobbing over George and Lennie, have admitted that even critics are only boys at heart, for that is just the mood that Mr. Steinbeck's work induces. So perhaps, again, they would admit that the secret of his success is that a certain simple type of reader feels, when he discovers that he has foreseen correctly any movement of a story, a kind of participation in the creative act of the author. Almost any critic would admit this if the book under consideration were one of the Tarzan books, or a book by Lloyd Douglas, or any one of a dozen "popular novelists" of the sort they affect to despise, but perhaps they have not noticed that the symmetry and expectedness (or, if you prefer, read "economy") of Mr. Steinbeck's work put the average pulp-writer to shame.

If Lennie kills a mouse by stroking it, you may be sure he will unintentionally kill something larger in the same way; when you hear of Curley's wife's soft hair, "like fur", you can begin to cooperate with the author by expectation of her end. When George learns that a poor old worthless smelly dog can be dispatched easily by a shot in the back of his head, you are unwarrantably guileless if you do not suspect the manner in which Lennie will meet his death. If an old man dreams of a home, peace, and security, you may be sure that a home, peace, and security are what he will most agonizingly just miss. And so forth. You can call this sort of foreshadowing "economy" if it pleases you; but if "economy" is the word you choose you should abandon the word "obvious" hereafter and forever.

It may be some time before the current vogue for Steinbeck passes. Masculine sentimentality, particularly when it masquerades as toughness, is a little longer in being seen through than the feminine or the inclusively human variety. Undoubtedly there are plenty who would deny, even today, that *The Sun Also Rises* and *What Price Glory?* are (although far more distinguished) prototypes of *Of Mice and Men.* Surely it should not be too hard to find the soft spots where the decay shows: the romantic overestimation of the rôle of friendship, the wax-figure women, bright, hard, treacherous, unreal—whether a Lady Brett, the French girl behind the lines, or "Curley's wife", these are all essentially hateful women, women from whom it is a virtue to flee to masculine companionship. There was certainly a sort of stag-party hysteria and uproar about the approval we have been hearing for this padded short story about underdogs and animals, bunkhouses and bathos, which has seldom risen so high since "Wait for baby!" soared over the footlights. . . . Ah, I was forgetting Mr. Chips.

> —Dorothea Brande Collins, "Reading at Random," *American Review* 11, No. 1 (April 1937): 104–6

❖

JOSEPH WOOD KRUTCH ON THE DRAMATIZATION OF *OF MICE AND MEN*

[Joseph Wood Krutch (1893–1970) was a prolific American critic and social commentator. Among his major works are *The Modern Temper* (1929), *Five Masters: A Study in the Mutations of the Novel* (1930), and biographies of Edgar Allan Poe (1926), Samuel Johnson (1944), and Henry David Thoreau (1948). In this extract, Krutch studies the play version of *Of Mice and Men* and believes that its sentimentality is what made it popular with readers and audiences alike.]

The story—difficult to tell without seeming to do it an intentional injustice—is concerned with a strange friendship between two migratory harvest workers, one of whom is a witless but amiable giant given to fondling all soft and helpless things with a hand so unintentionally heavy that, sooner or later, he infallibly breaks their necks. The theme is tenderness taking strange forms in a brutal environment, and the dramatic tension arises out of our foreknowledge of the fact that at some time and for some reason the heavy hand will be laid with fatal results upon the camp's only member of the female sex—a pathetic little nymphomaniac married to the boss's cruel son. All the grotesqueness inherent in the tale is emphasized rather than concealed (we first meet the strange pair when the giant is being unwillingly deprived of a dead mouse he has been keeping too long in his pocket), but the skill of the writing is such that the whole is carried off far better than one could well imagine and that success is absolute in so far as it consists merely in forcing the spectator to take the whole with perfect seriousness. The only question is whether he is right so to take it, whether what we are presented with is really a tale of eerie power and tenderness, or whether, as it seems to me, everything from beginning to end is completely "literary" in the bad sense and as shamelessly cooked up as, let us say, the death of Little Nell.

After all, Dickens, as well as thousands of his readers, sincerely believed that Little Nell was the real thing. A fascinating but largely unexplored field lies ready for any psychologist-critic who wishes to examine the reasons behind the demand of every age that sentiment be served up according to some formula, the peculiar charm of which no previous age would have recognized and which every succeeding age finds patently ridiculous. Your Victorian was ready to weep over the fate of any sentimental monster if that monster could be described in sufficiently convincing terms as "innocent." Today nothing arouses the suspicions of any audience more infallibly than either that word or that thing, but a tough Little Nell, thoroughly familiar with four-letter words, would be a sensation on any stage, and the moronic giant of Mr. Steinbeck seems real because all the accidents of his character and surroundings are violent and brutal. Mr. Steinbeck, as I have already suggested, writes with great technical adroitness. But neither that adroitness nor all the equal expertness of staging and acting exhibited in the peformance of his play would avail if the whole were not concocted according to a formula which happens to be at the moment infallible. Sentiment flavored with a *soupçon* of social criticism and labeled "Ruthless Realism" is well nigh certain to be applauded by thousands quite unaware that they are responding to an appeal as old—not as the theater itself—but as the rise of the middle-class public. Mr. Steinbeck's most

recent novel, *The Grapes of Wrath,* is written in quite a different style and may possibly indicate that he himself realizes the
extent to which *Of Mice and Men* was meretricious.
—Joseph Wood Krutch, *The American Drama Since 1918: An
Informal History* (New York: Random House, 1939), pp. 128–30

❖

HARRY THORNTON MOORE ON DRAMATIC ELEMENTS IN *OF MICE AND MEN*

[Harry Thornton Moore (1909–1981) was a leading
scholar of D. H. Lawrence; he edited many of
Lawrence's works and wrote an important biography,
The Priest of Love (1974). He taught for many years at
Southern Illinois University. In this extract from one of
the earliest book-length studies of Steinbeck, Moore
points out that even the short novel *Of Mice and Men*
is structured more like a play than a novel.]

Structurally, the novel was from the first a play: it is divided
into six parts, each part a scene—the reader may observe that
the action never moves away from a central point in each of
these units. Steinbeck's manner of writing was coming over
quite firmly to the dramatic. The process had begun in the latter part of *In Dubious Battle* (which the novelist John O'Hara
once tried unsuccessfully to dramatize), where some of the
most exciting happenings in the story take place offstage. After
Of Mice and Men was published and the suggestion was made
that it be prepared for the stage, Steinbeck said it could be produced directly from the book, as the earliest moving pictures
had been produced. It was staged in almost exactly this way in
the spring of 1937 by a labor-theater group in San Francisco,
and although the venture was not a failure it plainly demon-
strated to Steinbeck that the story needed to be adapted to
dramatic form. The San Francisco *Chronicle's* report of the performance admitted that the staged novel had power, though it
"seems slightly ill at ease in the theater . . . Its climaxes need
sharpening," for "some of the scenes end lamely, tapering off

without the pointed tag-lines that might crystallize or intensify the action. And there are certain passages of dialogue that caused embarrassed titters in the audience; it would do the play no harm to leave these out altogether." But when Steinbeck transferred the story into final dramatic form for the New York stage he took 85% of his lines bodily from the novel. A few incidents needed juggling, one or two minor new ones were introduced, and some (such as Lennie's imaginary speech with his Aunt Clara at the end of the novel) were omitted. A Hollywood studio bought the film rights to *Of Mice and Men,* but the picture has not been made yet.

Although there are few descriptive passages in the novel *Of Mice and Men,* Steinbeck's presentation of ranch life has once again the gleam of the living. The people, human beings reduced to bareness of speech and thought and action, are on the sidetracks of the main line of western culture. They exist in a hard reality, but most of them are susceptible to dreams. Some of them are lost in a compensatory dream-image of themselves, others are set afire by the wish-dream of George and Lennie. But in one way or another all the dreams and some of the people (the good along with the bad) are smashed. The spirit of doom prevails as strongly as in the pages of Hardy or of Steinbeck's fellow-Californian, Robinson Jeffers.

—Harry Thornton Moore, *The Novels of John Steinbeck: A First Critical Study* (Chicago: Normandie House, 1939), pp. 48–50

❖

MAXWELL GEISMAR ON LENNIE

[Maxwell Geismar (1909–1979) was a leading American critic and biographer. Among his books are *American Moderns, from Rebellion to Conformity* (1958), *Henry James and the Jacobites* (1963), and *Mark Twain: An American Prophet* (1970). In this extract, Geismar, tracing the figure of Lennie in previous works by Steinbeck, criticizes the character for being theatrical and infantile.]

Half fairy, as it were, and half elephant, Lennie is of course the chief of the impositions upon our literary tolerance. Steinbeck, to be sure, has been interested previously in these grotesque and delightfully demented beings. Tularecito, the talented gnome of *The Pastures of Heaven,* is one of them. There is again Johnny Bear, who, combining with the weird ancient of *To a God Unknown,* becomes our own Lennie. Lennie, in fact, is merely Steinbeck's 'Secret' embodied in a rather perverse hobgoblin. What is the meaning of this line of mystic brutes? Do they, like monkeys, obscene but illuminating, perform in public what we consider in private, the materialization of our inner desires, a little more in evidence, perhaps, but no more queer? There are other possible significances, certainly, but there is little evidence that Steinbeck means them to be other than what they seem, and we are forced to conclude that, in terms of Steinbeck's past, Lennie and his brothers are again more theatrical than evocative. The peculiar, like the ordinary, is the legitimate province of the writer, but it is precisely his function to make it legitimate, to portray it for its illumination on the entire context of human activity. As the writer on human oddities, Steinbeck, rather than meditating upon his creations, merely exhibits them. Rather like the barker in a side-circus, he exhorts us to enter and do no more than gape upon poor Lennie; a barker, I am almost obliged to add, himself rather enthralled by the abnormality, and who, after the last sightseer, comes in to gaze in person.

In *Of Mice and Men,* moreover, Steinbeck uses Lennie to carry his familiar element of violence, the semi-sadism which, appearing most clearly in *To a God Unknown,* now fills the play: of which the shooting of Candy's dog is a crucial example, and that of Lennie himself is the climax. Both of these executions are wonderful stage and logically unnecessary. The dog would have probably preferred, like most of us, slumber however fitful to eternal rest; and the more civilized solution of the play would have been to take Lennie to an asylum, where indeed, some may argue, he belonged before the play opened. If I seem to stress this infantile and illogical brutality, which is the core of the play, it is simply because Steinbeck himself does. And where these elements were restrained in the early work of Steinbeck, here they are exploited, made commercial and theatrical; here, in brief, is Steinbeck's past pushed to its limit, the end of the road.

—Maxwell Geismar, "John Steinbeck: Of Wrath or Joy," *Writers in Crisis: The American Novel Between Two Wars* (Boston: Houghton Mifflin, 1942), pp. 257–58

❖

Peter Lisca on Why George Stays with Lennie

[Peter Lisca (b. 1925), a former professor of English at the University of Florida, is a leading scholar on Steinbeck, having written *The Wide World of John Steinbeck* (1958) and *John Steinbeck: Nature and Myth* (1978). In this extract, Lisca notes that George's reasons for remaining with the hapless Lennie may reside in George's psychology—that Lennie may be a rationalization for George's sense of failure in life.]

Almost every character in the story asks George why he goes around with Lennie: the foreman, Curley, Slim, and Candy. Crooks, the lonely Negro, doesn't ask but he does speculate about it, and shrewdly—" 'a guy talkin' to another guy and it don't make no difference if he don't hear or understand. The thing is, they're talkin' . . .' " George's explanations vary from outright lies to a simple statement of " 'We travel together.' " It is only to Slim, the superior workman with the "God-like eyes," that he tells a great part of the truth. Among other reasons, such as his feeling of responsibility for Lennie in return for the latter's unfailing loyalty, and their having grown up together, there is revealed another: " 'He's dumb as hell, but he ain't crazy. An' I ain't so bright neither, or I wouldn't be buckin' barley for my fifty and found. If I was even a little bit smart, I'd have my own place, an' I'd be bringin' in my own crops, 'sted of doin' all the work and not getting what comes up outa the ground.' "

This statement, together with George's repeatedly expressed desire to take his fifty bucks to a cat house and his continual playing of solitaire, reveals that to some extent George needs Lennie as a rationalization for his failure. This is one of the reasons why, after the murder of Curley's wife, George refuses Candy's offer of a partnership which would have made the dream of a "safe place" a reality. The dream of the farm originates with Lennie; and it is only through Lennie, who also makes it impossible, that the dream has any meaning for George. An understanding of this dual relationship will do much to mitigate the frequent charge that Steinbeck's depiction of George's attachment is concocted of pure sentimentality. At the end of the novel, George's going off with Slim to "do the town" is more than an escape from grief. It is an ironic and symbolic twist to his dream.

> —Peter Lisca, "Motif and Pattern in *Of Mice and Men*," *Modern Fiction Studies* 2, No. 4 (Winter 1956–57): 233–34

❖

WARREN FRENCH ON *OF MICE AND MEN* AS A COMEDY

[Warren French (b. 1922) has taught at several universities, including Purdue and the University of Missouri. He is the author of *J. D. Salinger* (1976), *John Steinbeck's Fiction, Revisited* (1994), and many other volumes. In this extract from his earlier study of Steinbeck, French argues that *Of Mice and Men* is not a tragedy at all but instead a "dark comedy" about man's acceptance of his own mediocrity.]

Despite the grim events it chronicles *Of Mice and Men* is not a tragedy, but a comedy—which, if it were Shakespearean, we would call a "dark comedy"—about the triumph of the indomitable will to survive. This is a story not of man's defeat at the hands of an implacable nature, but of man's painful conquest of this nature and of his difficult, conscious rejection of his dreams of greatness and acceptance of his own mediocrity. Unfortunately, the allegory is less clear in the play version than in the novel, since Steinbeck, probably to provide a more effective curtain, eliminates George's last conversation with

Slim and ends with the shooting of Lennie. The original ending would also probably have been too involved for playgoers to follow after experiencing the emotions engendered by the climactic episodes.

Lennie has been viewed sometimes as an example of Steinbeck's preoccupation with subhuman types; actually Lennie is not a character in the story at all, but rather a device like a golden coin in *Moby Dick* to which the other characters may react in a way that allows the reader to perceive their attitudes. So intensely focused upon the relationship between George and Lennie is the novel that the other characters are likely to be overlooked; yet each makes an important contribution to the narrative and provides a clue to Steinbeck's conception of the human condition.

The protest against racial discrimination and the treatment of the aged through the characters of Crooks and Candy needs no elaboration. The symbolism of Curley and his ill-fated bride is perhaps summed up in her statement that they married after she "met him out to Riverside Dance Palace that same night." There is a sordid echo of Fitzgerald and the "lost generation" here; for, like the Buchanans in *The Great Gatsby*, these are "careless people" who smash up things and "let other people clean up the mess." It is true that the girl is smashed up herself, but, unlike Curley, she did have dreams and disappointments. He simply, like the Buchanans, retreats into his "vast carelessness." The wife, not George, is the one in the novel who is destroyed when, instead of controlling her dreams, she allows them to control her; and Curley, not Lennie, is actually the willfully animalistic type.

The most interesting characters—except for George and Lennie—are Carlson and Slim, two other ranch hands, who have the last words in the novel. They are complements, symbolizing, on one hand, the insensitive and brutal; on the other, the kindly and perceptive. "Now what the hell ya suppose is eatin' them two guys?" are Carlson's words—the last in the book—as Slim and George sadly walk off for a drink. Undoubtedly this sums up Steinbeck's concept of an unperceptive world's reaction to the drama just enacted. The uncomprehending responses to his books had given Steinbeck sufficient

grounds for being aware of this "practical" attitude and through Carlson he strikes back at the men to whom Doctor Burton in *In Dubious Battle* attributes the world's "wild-eyed confusion." But Steinbeck also suggests that such men have the last word.
—Warren French, *John Steinbeck* (New York: Twayne, 1961), pp. 76–77

❖

F. W. WATT ON THE CHARACTERS IN *OF MICE AND MEN*

[F. W. Watt (b. 1927) is a British literary critic who has coedited *Essays in English Literature from the Renaissance to the Victorian Age* (1964) and written a study of Steinbeck, from which this extract is taken. Here, Watt argues that the relationship of George and Lennie rises above sentimentality because of its reciprocal nature, but that the absence of depth in other characters makes the book seem thin.]

George has the responsibility of caring for Lennie as though he were a child, but dangerous as no child could be: allowing him to express his inarticulate desires by petting a mouse or a puppy, but not a woman's dress or her hair—for women mistake his intentions, with disastrous results. Without George's watchful eye on him he will kill what he touches, mouse, puppy, or woman, in trying to express his feelings. "God a' mighty," George tells him in disgust as they camp on a riverbank; "if I was alone I could live so easy. I could go get a job an' work, an' no trouble. No mess at all, and when the end of the month come I could take my fifty bucks and go into town and get whatever I want. Why, I could stay in a cat house all night. I could eat anyplace I want, hotel or any place, and order any damn thing I could think of. An' I could do that every damn month. Get a gallon of whiskey, or set in a pool room and play cards or shoot pool." This is George's dream of freedom, and he returns to it frequently when the frustration of taking care of Lennie is too much for him.

But over against this is another dream, one which he shares with Lennie; they speak of it by the river as the novel begins, and again at the pathetic conclusion. The telling of it is a ritual game they play together. "Guys like us, that work on ranches," George says, "are the loneliest guys in the world," without family, home, or anyone who cares about them. But George and Lennie stick together, help each other, and are working for a purpose:

> 'Someday—we're gonna get the jack together and gonna have a little house and a couple of acres an' a cow and some pigs and—'
> '*An live off the fatta the lan*',' Lennie shouted. 'An' have *rabbits*. Go on, George! Tell about what we're gonna have in the garden and about the rabbits in the cages and about the rain in the winter and the stove, and how thick the cream is on the milk like you can hardly cut it. Tell about that, George. . . .'

This is the "best-laid scheme" and the "promised joy" which is ruined when Lennie once again kills something he is trying to show love—the daughter-in-law of their new employer—and George is obliged to shoot him to keep him from being lynched. George is left with the free life he claimed to want, but which he actually dreaded, recognising, though never admitting, its utter futility and loneliness.

It is the reciprocal nature of the relationship between Lennie and George that rescues it from sentimentality and makes it convincing. Undoubtedly some of the lesser characters appear rather more theatrical in conception: the crippled Negro stable-hand Crook, and Candy, the old swamper, who both attach themselves to George's and Lennie's Adamic dream; and Curley's sluttish wife, the Eve who occasions the destruction of all the men's hopes. They are fitted competently enough into the action, but the slenderness of the central theme, the lack of a dense social context, and the artificiality that increases the farther removed we are from the Lennie-George relationship account for Steinbeck's feeling that the book was "thin" and "brittle."

—F. W. Watt, *John Steinbeck* (New York: Grove, 1962), pp. 60–61

❖

WILLIAM GOLDHURST ON THE CAIN AND ABEL THEME IN *OF MICE AND MEN*

[William Goldhurst (b. 1929) teaches in the department of humanities at the University of Florida. He is the author of *F. Scott Fitzgerald and His Contemporaries* (1963). In this extract, Goldhurst believes that the theme of Cain and Abel is the central guiding principle of *Of Mice and Men*.]

Viewed in the light of its mythic and allegorical implications, *Of Mice and Men* is a story about the nature of man's fate in a fallen world, with particular emphasis upon the question: is man destined to live alone, a solitary wanderer on the face of the earth, or is it the fate of man to care for man, to go his way in companionship with another? This is the same theme that occurs in the Old Testament, as early as Chapter Four of Genesis, immediately following the Creation and Expulsion. In effect, the question Steinbeck poses is the same question Cain poses to the Lord: "Am I my brother's keeper." From its position in the Scriptural version of human history we may assume with the compilers of the early books of the Bible that it is the primary *question concerning man as he is,* after he has lost the innocence and non-being of Eden. It is the same question that Steinbeck chose as the theme of his later book *East of Eden* (1952), in which novel the Cain and Abel story is reenacted in a contemporary setting and where, for emphasis, Steinbeck has his main characters read the Biblical story aloud and comment upon it, climaxing the discussion with the statement made by Lee: "I think this is the best-known story in the world because it is everybody's story. I think it is the symbol story of the human soul." *Of Mice and Men* is an early Steinbeck variation on this symbol story of the human soul. The implications of the Cain-and-Abel drama are everywhere apparent in the fable of George and Lennie and provide its mythic vehicle.

Contrary to Lee's confident assertion, however, most people know the Cain and Abel story only in general outline. The details of the drama need to be filled in, particularly for the purpose of seeing how they apply to Steinbeck's novella. Cain was a farmer, Adam and Eve's first-born son. His offerings of agricultural produce to the Lord failed to find favor, whereas the livestock offered by Cain's brother, Abel, was well received. Angry, jealous, and rejected Cain killed Abel when they were working in the field, and when the Lord inquired of Cain, where is your brother, Cain replied: "I know not: Am I my brother's keeper." For his crime of homicide the Lord banished Cain from His company and from the company of his parents and set upon him a particular curse, the essence of which was that Cain was to become homeless, a wanderer, and an agricultural worker who would never possess or enjoy the fruits of his labor. Cain was afraid that other men would hear of his crime and try to kill him, but the Lord marked him in a certain way so as to preserve him from the wrath of others. Thus Cain left home and went to the land of Nod, which the story tells us lies east of Eden.

The drama of Cain finds its most relevant application in *Of Mice and Men* in the relationship between Lennie and George, and in the other characters' reactions to their associations. In the first of his six scenes Steinbeck establishes the two ideas that will be developed throughout. The first of these is the affectionate symbiosis of the two protagonists, their brotherly mutual concern and faithful companionship. Steinbeck stresses the beauty, joy, security, and comfort these two derive from the relationship:

> "If them other guys gets in jail they can rot for all anybody gives a damn. But not us."
> Lennie broke in, "But not us! An' why? Because . . . because I got you to look after me and you got me to look after you, and that's why." He laughed delightedly.

The second idea, which is given equal emphasis, is the fact that this sort of camaraderie is rare, different, almost unique in the world George and Lennie inhabit; other men, in contrast to these two, are solitary souls without friends or companions. Says George in Scene One:

> "Guys like us, that work on ranches, are the loneliest guys in the world. They got no family. They don't belong no place. They come to a ranch an' work up a stake and then they go into town and blow their stakes, and the first thing you know they're poundin' their tail on some other ranch."

The alternative to the George-Lennie companionship is Aloneness, made more dreadful by the addition of an economic futility that Steinbeck augments and reinforces in later sections. The migratory ranch worker, in other words, is the fulfillment of the Lord's curse on Cain: "When thou tillest the ground, it shall not henceforth yield unto thee her strength; a fugitive and vagabond shalt thou be in the earth." Steinbeck's treatment of the theme is entirely free from a sense of contrivance; all the details in *Of Mice and Men* seem natural in the context and organically related to the whole; but note that in addition to presenting Lennie and George as men who till the ground and derive no benefits from their labor, he also manages to have them "on the run" when they are introduced in the first scene—this no doubt to have his main characters correspond as closely as possible to the Biblical passage: "a fugitive and a vagabond shalt thou be. . . ."

—William Goldhurst, "*Of Mice and Men:* John Steinbeck's Parable of the Curse of Cain," *Western American Literature* 6, No. 2 (Summer 1971): 126–28

❖

HOWARD LEVANT ON THE SIMPLICITY OF *OF MICE AND MEN*

[Howard Levant (b. 1929), who has taught at Hartwick College and Pepperdine University, has edited *The Writer and the World* (1976) and written *The Novels of John Steinbeck* (1974), from which this extract is taken. Here, Levant argues that *Of Mice and Men* is built upon a deliberately simple plan, but the result is that the novel is too much under Steinbeck's control and fails to come alive.]

Everything in the development of the novel is designed to contribute to a simplification of character and event.

The opening scene of the green pool in the Salinas River promises serenity, but in the final scene the pool is the background for Lennie's violent death. George's initial hope that

Lennie can hide his flawed humanity by seeming to be conventional is shattered in the end. Lennie's flaw grows into a potential for evil, and every evil is ascribed to him after his unwitting murder of Curley's wife. The objective image of the good life in the future, "a little house and a couple of acres an' a cow and some pigs," is opposed sharply to the present sordid reality of the bunkhouse and the ranch. Minor characters remain little more than opposed types, identifiable by allegorical tags. Curley is the unsure husband, opposed to and fearful of his sluttish, unnamed wife. Slim is a minor god in his perfect mastery of his work. His serenity is contrasted sharply with Curley's hysterical inability to please or to control his wife, and it contrasts as easily with the wife's constant, obvious discontent. Candy and Crooks are similar types, men without love. Both are abused by Curley, his wife, and the working crew. (Lennie might fall into this category of defenselessness, if he were aware enough to realize the situation; but he is not.) These sharp oppositions and typed personae restrict the development of the novel. The merely subordinate characters, such as Carlson and Whit, who only begin or fill out a few scenes, are strictly nonhuman, since they remain abstract instruments within a design.

The climax of that design is simplified in its turn, since it serves only to manipulate Lennie into a moral situation beyond his understanding. The climax is doubled, a pairing of opposites. In its first half, when Curley's wife attempts to seduce Lennie as a way to demonstrate her hatred of Curley, Lennie is content (in his nice innocence) to stroke her soft hair; but he is too violent, and he snaps her neck in a panic miscalculation as he tries to force her to be quiet. In the second half, George shoots Lennie to prevent a worse death at the hands of others. The melodramatic quality of these events will be considered at a later point. Here, it is more important to observe, in the design, that the climax pairs an exploration of the ambiguity of love in the rigid contrast between the different motives that activate Curley's wife and George. Curley's wife wants to use Lennie to show her hatred for Curley; George shoots Lennie out of a real affection for him. The attempted seduction balances the knowing murder; both are disastrous expressions of love. Lennie is the unknowing center of the design in both halves of this climax. Steinbeck's control is all too evident. There is not much sense of dramatic illumination because the quality of the paired climax is that of a mechanical problem of joining two parallels. Lennie's necessary passivity enforces the quality of a mechanical design. He is only the man to whom things happen. Being so limited, he is incapable of providing that sudden widening insight which alone justifies an artist's extreme dependence on a rigid design. Therefore, in general, *Of Mice and Men* remains a simple anecdote.

> —Howard Levant, "*Of Mice and Men*," *The Novels of John Steinbeck: A Critical Study* (Columbia: University of Missouri Press, 1974), pp. 135–37

❖

Nelson Valjean on the Dramatic Production of *Of Mice and Men*

[Nelson Valjean (b. 1901) is the author of *John Steinbeck: The Errant Knight* (1975), from which the following extract is taken. Here, Valjean discusses the writing of the novel version of *Of Mice and Men* and then its adaptation into a play, written in collaboration with George S. Kaufman.]

Intrigued by the thought of writing a play, [Steinbeck] hoped to do a story which he could call "a novel to be played," one that could be lifted, almost intact, from the printed page to the stage. Dialogue would be typical bunkhouse talk, scenic background would be held to a minimum. Soon he fell to work on "Something That Happened," a title later changed to *Of Mice and Men.* Two months' work had gone into it when his setter pup, Toby, left alone one night, ripped into the manuscript, turning much of it into confetti. He rewrote.

In May 1937, *Of Mice and Men* had its national premiere at the Green Street Playhouse in San Francisco under the auspices of the San Francisco Theater Union. Newspaper critics saw the stage portrayal of the two lonely and inarticulate ranch hands as poignant and fairly effective. The play was well received but certainly not wildly acclaimed. Obviously doctoring was needed.

That same spring, now financially able to travel, the Steinbecks took a freighter to New York, via the Panama Canal, where John visited his agents, squirmed into a borrowed suit to attend a dinner party, and signed a contract for the filming of *Of Mice and Men*. A European trip followed, and the Steinbecks were back in New York again by early August. John immediately went to work with George S. Kaufman on a project delayed by the European jaunt—a dramatization of *Of Mice and Men*. At Kaufman's farm in Bucks County, Pennsylvania, the noted playwright turned adviser and consultant, expressing his enthusiasm for the way the novel lent itself to the stage.

"Kaufman would be reading over the lines to me and suddenly he'd stop," Steinbeck said later. "He can tell ahead of time just when an audience is going to suppress a titter or when it will burst into a belly-laugh or when it will remain completely silent. The man's a marvel." While Kaufman didn't write a line of the dialogue, his suggestions were invaluable.

Finishing the play, and after helping interview eighty applicants for the roles of Lennie and George but without waiting for opening night, John wearily headed for the West Coast, anxious to get home and start another farmland story, then in its planning and early writing stages. Contrary to long-perpetuated myths, he did not tarry to join the Okies and Arkies on their migration westward.

Did he ever worry how New York would accept his *Mice* drama? At about six o'clock on the evening of November 23, 1937, he admitted, he felt his stomach slowly turning around as he realized the curtain had just risen on the first act at New York's Music Box Theatre. There was no reason to worry. Audiences cried openly and beat their hands deafeningly. Critics were enraptured. The play ran through April, when it was awarded the New York Drama Critics' silver plaque as the best American play to be produced in a New York theatre during the 1937–38 season.

Interviewed at his home, Steinbeck denied there were any subtle implications in the play. "All I tried to write was the story of two Salinas Valley vagrants," he said. "It hasn't any meaning or special significance outside of what appears on the surface. It's just a story. I don't know what it means, if anything, and damned if I care. My business is only storytelling."

—Nelson Valjean, *John Steinbeck: The Errant Knight* (San Francisco: Chronicle Books, 1975), pp.158–60

❖

Sunita Jain on Evil in *Of Mice and Men*

[Sunita Jain (b. 1941), an Indian literary critic, has written *John Steinbeck's Concept of Man* (1979), from which the following extract is taken. Here, Jain studies the role of evil in Steinbeck's short novel, declaring that Lennie is both a victim and an agent of destruction.]

Several factors in the novel are responsible for its extremely powerful drama: *Of Mice and Men* tells of simple dreams of simple people like Lennie, George, Candy, Crooks—the dreams that make us sympathize with the characters—but it also contains larger forces that destroy these dreams; however, when the destruction takes place no one factor can be held responsible. This refusal on the author's part to delineate evil, plus a totally objective point of view, keeps the novel from becoming just a protest novel, and keeps the portraits of George and Lennie from becoming sentimental. In fact, the balance between narrative material, themes, and form in this novel is so intricate that when Lennie dies at the end of the novel, one cannot say that Lennie's death was caused by a "tart" or by the jealous nature of a "mean" fellow by the name of Curley. Similarly, no one can say that Lennie's own feeble mind and his brute strength bring about his ruin. All these elements contribute, no doubt, but no one can make any of these, or even a group of these elements, solely responsible for Lennie's death. Besides, Lennie's death is not even the tragedy of the novel. The tragedy is not that Lennie has to die; the tragedy is that George has to go on living after having killed Lennie. The posse searching for Lennie could have lynched him, or Curley could have mutilated him, but all this has happened before. It is only when a man has to kill a part of himself, his "inarticulate yearning," that man realizes he is God only in his aspirations and dreams. In reality, he must go on living like an animal, eating, working, mating, and sleeping. ⟨. . .⟩

Steinbeck has questioned life in *Of Mice and Men,* but as in his previous novel, *In Dubious Battle,* no easy scapegoats for evil are provided. Lennie, for example, is not only a victim in the novel, he is also the instrument of destruction, just as the strikers were in *In Dubious Battle.* The reader's attitude toward Lennie is one of ambivalence. The ambivalence keeps the novel from becoming melodramatic. Similarly, George is a tragic character like Jim Nolan in *In Dubious Battle.* George, like Jim, is blown faceless by the bullet that shot Lennie. From now on he will take his "fifty bucks" and spend his nights in "lousy cathouses." He will be like every bindle stiff in the country—a mean and lonely guy who has not found anything meaningful in life. George's living death, then, is the real tragedy in this novel.

However, the fact that Slim understands and validates the necessity of killing Lennie and the fact that George at the end of the novel is paired with Slim who has "god like eyes" indicates the beginning of a new and final phase in Steinbeck's novels. The novels, after *Of Mice and Men,* dramatize man's success in his efforts to impose order on his dual existence as an individual and as a group animal. Man, in novels such as *The Red Pony, The Grapes of Wrath,* attains dignity by becoming an effective group animal and a distinct individual.

—Sunita Jain, *John Steinbeck's Concept of Man: A Critical Study of His Novels* (New Delhi: New Statesman Publishing Co., 1979), pp. 38–39, 42

❖

PAUL MCCARTHY ON *OF MICE AND MEN* AS COMPARED TO *IN DUBIOUS BATTLE*

[Paul McCarthy (b. 1921) teaches in the department of humanities at Northern Seattle Community College. He is the editor of *Long Fiction of the American Renaissance: A Symposium on Genre* (1979) and the author of *"The Twisted Mind": Madness in Herman Melville's Fiction* (1990). In this extract, taken from his book on Steinbeck, McCarthy compares *Of Mice and Men* with its predecessor, *In Dubious Battle* (1936), finding in the former less emphasis on the political and more on the personal.]

Of Mice and Men and *In Dubious Battle* differ in that the former lacks widespread violence, class conflict, and Marxian ideology. They are similar in that the characters have working-class backgrounds and the story is set on large California ranches during the Depression. Conditions in *Of Mice and Men* do appear less grim, but they are hardly reassuring or normal. Men must go from ranch to ranch to work for their "50 and found." Lennie and George, who find a place through "Murray and Ready's," an employment agency of some kind, are treated like numbers: they receive work slips and bus tickets. Like others they carry their few possessions in a blanket, or "bindle," and are called "bindle stiffs" by Curley's wife. The fifty-dollar salary does not last long, for, as George confesses only too sadly, it can disappear in a Saturday night in town, the only genuine relief from the monotony of farm work. So the men keep moving, and most with no hope whatsoever. As George explains to both himself and sidekick Lennie,

> Guys like us, that work on ranches, are the loneliest guys in the world. They got no family. They don't belong no place. They . . . work up a stake and . . . blow their stake, and the first thing you know they're poundin' their tail on some other ranch. They ain't got nothing to look ahead to.

But in this novel of hard knocks and low pay, characters have a few things to look forward to. A man can usually find work at fifty dollars per month, plus room and board, which is better than the fifteen or twenty cents per hour the strikers in Torgas

Valley might receive. If a migrant is steady and reliable, he could possibly stay on indefinitely at a ranch. His search for security could end there as it has for Carlson, who can put in eleven hours daily bucking barley and worry about nothing. Of course, like others Carlson has nothing to dream about, either. Another possibility, realized by few, is represented by Slim, the jerkline skinner, "capable of driving ten, sixteen, even twenty mules with a single line to the leaders." Among ranch workers Slim has reached the top. He has unusual skill with wagons and mules, knows all phases of ranch work, and is the acknowledged leader wherever he may be. Having no conflict or doubts, Slim is not looking for something better. He seemingly has no dreams.

The dream itself is the final possibility. This is not the elaborate communist dream of Mac and Jim in *In Dubious Battle,* but the personal, limited dream of two drifters like George and Lennie. One essential for such a dream, particularly its realization, is friendship, and that too must be of a special kind. There are friendships on the ranch—of Slim and Carlson, Candy and Crooks—but these are either temporary or ordinary. The friendship of George and Lennie, which goes back many years, is based on various needs. The mentally retarded Lennie, who cannot survive on his own, needs the protection and guidance of someone like George. Without George, Lennie would run off to a cave in the hills, as he sometimes threatens to do, or find himself in an institution. The comparatively self-sufficient George complains regularly about Lennie's stupidity and helplessness. Complaining can take the edge off the monotony and loneliness of ranch life; it can also enhance his sense of superiority. But afterwards George feels guilty about getting angry at Lennie, and he feels also a grudging affection that he would not openly admit. Lennie in turn has come to love the person who is all things to him.

—Paul McCarthy, *John Steinbeck* (New York: Ungar, 1980), pp. 57–59

❖

[John H. Timmerman (b. 1945), a professor of English at Calvin College, is the author of *Other Worlds: The Fantasy Genre* (1983), *The Dramatic Landscapes of Steinbeck's Short Stories* (1990), and *T. S. Eliot's Ariel Poems: The Poetics of Recovery* (1994). In this extract from his book on Steinbeck's fiction, Timmerman finds that *Of Mice and Men* is tightly unified in its theme and imagery.]

Of Mice and Men is one of Steinbeck's most compressed and unified works. Nonetheless, it achieves an artistic richness of structure and theme that ranks it among the best of his works. Three items in particular distinguish the novel: the framing and foreshadowing through structure, the development of Lennie's character and the theme of friendship, and the nature of human dreams.

The novel opens with the objective specificity of locale that would mark stage directions, or perhaps cinema. Like a long pan of the camera, the opening scene traces the Salinas River where it "drops in close to the hillside bank and runs deep and green" near Soledad. Following the flow of the river, the scene narrows and becomes more specific in detail, moving from the broad expanse of the "golden foothill slopes" of the Gabilan Mountains to the very small setting of "the sandy bank under the trees," where we find details as minute as "a lizard makes a great skittering" and "the split-wedge tracks of deer." The narrowing vision provides a smooth and gentle transition to the two bindlestiffs hunkered by a fire in the evening of the day. The light, too, narrows and focuses, from the broad, golden flanks of the Gabilans to the evening duskiness and the shade "that climbed up the hills toward the top."

The expertly framed opening is precisely echoed and inverted at the close of the novel, where the same two bindlestiffs stand by "the deep green pool of the Salinas River" in the evening of the day. Once again shade pushes the sunlight "up the slopes of the Gabilan Mountains, and the hilltops were rosy in the sun." We find the same, familiarly routine skitterings of birds and animals by the sandy bank, only now a small something has happened. The original title of the novel, "Something That Happened," is precisely the point here; a small thing occurs, however momentous and tragic in the lives of Lennie and George, that goes virtually unnoticed in the ways of the world. Antonia Seixas comments in her article "John Steinbeck and the Non-Teleological Bus" that "the hardest task a writer can set himself is to tell the story of 'something that happened' without explaining 'why'—and make it convincing and moving." Again, as if viewing the scene through a movie camera, we observe the "what" without the explanatory "why." While Lennie stares into the sun-washed mountains, George recreates the dream as he levels the Luger at the base of Lennie's skull.

The mountains that frame the story, as they frame the little thing that happened in the lives of George and Lennie, always carry large significance for Steinbeck. In *The Grapes of Wrath* crossing the mountains represents the entrance into the promised land for the Okies. In *East of Eden,* Steinbeck provides two mountain ranges, one dark and one light, which symbolically frame the struggle between good and evil in the valley between those ranges. In *The Red Pony,* as in *To a God Unknown,* the mountains represent mystery; in the former work old Gitano goes to the mountains on Easter to die; in the latter Joseph Wayne witnesses strange, ancient rituals. In *Of Mice and Men* also, the darkening mountains represent the mystery of death, carefully sustained in the minor imagery of the heron seizing and eating the little water snakes.

In between the two scenes of the mountains on those two evenings, and in the serene willow grove that, as Peter Lisca points out, symbolizes "a retreat from the world to a primeval innocence," we have the quiet drama of George and Lennie's dream unfolding and unraveling. But this dream is doomed, and Steinbeck provides ample foreshadowing in the novel, most notably in Candy's dog. According to Carlson, Candy's dog has to die because he is a cripple, out of sorts with the normal routine of society, something in the way. With careful detail Carlson describes how he would shoot the dog so that it would not feel any pain: " 'The way I'd shoot him, he wouldn't feel nothing. I'd put the gun right there.' He pointed with his toe. 'Right back of the head. He wouldn't even quiver.' "

Candy's huge regret is that he didn't do so himself. It would have been kinder to have the dog die by a familiar and loved hand than to have a stranger drag him to his death. The same feeling motivates George as he leads the social cripple Lennie to his dream world. For Steinbeck this act constitutes a rare heroism. Years later he wrote in a letter to Annie Laurie Williams ⟨August 28, 1957⟩:

> M & M may seem to be unrelieved tragedy, but it is not. A careful reading will show that while the audience knows, against its hopes, that the dream will not come true, the protagonists must, during the play, become convinced that it will come true. Everyone in the world has a dream he knows can't come off but he spends his life hoping it may. This is at once the sadness, the greatness and the triumph of our species. And this belief on stage must go from skepticism to possibility to probability before it is nipped off by whatever the modern word for fate is. And in hopelessness—George is able to rise to greatness—to kill his friend to save him. George is a hero and only heroes are worth writing about.

> —John Timmerman, *John Steinbeck's Fiction: The Aesthetics of the Road Taken* (Norman: University of Oklahoma Press, 1986), pp. 96–98

❖

ANNE LOFTIS ON THE HISTORICAL BACKGROUND OF *OF MICE AND MEN*

[Anne Loftis, a social critic and historian, is the author of *California—Where the Twain Did Meet* (1973) and coauthor of *The Great Betrayal: The Evacuation of the Japanese-Americans During World War II* (1969) and *A Long Time Coming: The Struggle to Urbanize America's Farm Workers* (1977). In this extract, Loftis places *Of Mice and Men* in its historical context, exploring the social and economic conditions of California in the 1930s.]

Steinbeck wrote *Of Mice and Men* midway through the 1930s, the most creative decade of his career. During this time he was becoming increasingly concerned about current social and economic problems in California, and he published three successive novels about farm workers, each distinctive in tone and conception.

Of Mice and Men was a deliberate change from his previous book, *In Dubious Battle* (1936), an imaginative interpretation of a contemporary farm strike and a study of the movement and action of crowds. In the new project he set out to work within a narrow framework, concentrating on a small number of characters in carefully detailed settings, telling his story as economically and dramatically as possible. He explained that he was teaching himself to write for the theater, and in fact he soon did translate the novel into a play.

The subject was less controversial than that of his previous book. He was writing about people who were isolated in the society of their time, who belonged to a group that was fast disappearing from the American scene. Only a short time before, thousands of itinerant single men had roamed the Western states following the harvests. Their labor was essential to the success of the bonanza grain-growing enterprises that had been started in the second half of the nineteenth century and had proliferated so rapidly that by the year 1900 some 125,000 threshers were migrating along a "belt" that extended from the Brazos Bottoms in Texas north to Saskatchewan and Manitoba, and from Minnesota west to the state of Washington. Many of them traveled by rail, arriving in the fields in empty boxcars that were later used to transport the grain.

In the early years they were paid an average wage of $2.50 to $3 a day plus board and room. The "room" was frequently a tent: living conditions were spartan. But wages rose at the time of the First World War when the price of wheat was high, partly through the action of the Industrial Workers of the World, which established an eight-hundred-mile picket line across the Great Plains states.

In California, where grain was the chief farm commodity in the 1870s and 1880s before the advent of irrigated agriculture, some of the early harvesters were disappointed miners returning from the goldfields. In the social and occupational hierarchy they were on a level considerably below the mule drivers, who, like Steinbeck's character Slim, were valued for their skill in handling as many as twenty animals "with a single line" and who were generally employed permanently on the ranches.

Steinbeck's recognition of the status of the mule driver epitomizes his re-creation of a working culture that was undergoing a historic change even as he wrote about it. In 1938, the year after *Of Mice and Men* was published, about half the nation's grain was harvested by mechanical combines that enabled 5 men to do the work that had been done formerly by 350. The single farm workers who traveled from job to job by train, or like George and Lennie by bus, were disappearing. They were being replaced by whole families migrating in cars, like the people in Steinbeck's next novel, *The Grapes of Wrath.*

—Anne Loftis, "A Historical Introduction to *Of Mice and Men,*" *The Short Novels of John Steinbeck,* ed. Jackson J. Benson (Durham: Duke University Press, 1990), pp. 39–40

❖

CHARLOTTE COOK HADELLA ON ILLUSION AND THE AMERICAN DREAM

[Charlotte Cook Hadella is a professor of English at Southern Oregon State College. In this extract, Hadella argues that the subject of *Of Mice and Men* is the power of illusion as it relates to the American dream.]

Since the subject of *Of Mice and Men,* on one level at least, is the destructive power of illusion as it pertains particularly to the American Dream, mythical discourse naturally influences the story. Critics have noted that the Garden of Eden myth "looms large" in *Of Mice and Men,* and Steinbeck appropriates Edenic elements to convey his personal interpretation of the American Dream. The role of woman in the Edenic framework, of course, is that of the temptress, the despoiler of the Garden. That Steinbeck manipulates his story to encompass the mythical interpretation is clear. In a *New York Times* interview in December 1937, while discussing his sources for characters and incidents in *Of Mice and Men,* Steinbeck claimed that he had witnessed Lennie's real-life counterpart's killing of a man, not a woman: "I was a bindle-stiff myself for quite a spell. I worked in the same country that the story is laid in. The characters are composites to a certain extent. Lennie was a real person. He's in an insane asylum in California right now. I worked alongside him for many weeks. He didn't kill a girl. He killed a ranch foreman. Got sore because the boss had fired his pal and stuck a pitchfork right through his stomach. I hate to tell you how many times I saw him do it. We couldn't stop him until it was too late."

To fit the mythical framework of his story, Steinbeck changes Lennie's victim from a man to a woman. Although George and Lennie's illusion of an Edenic existence would have been shattered just as surely if Lennie had killed Curley, for instance, instead of Curley's wife, Steinbeck makes the woman the instrument of destruction of the land dream. The mythical discourse of the fiction dictates that a woman precipitate the exile from paradise. Consequently, George espouses this concept of womanhood and accepts Candy's assessment of Curley's wife as a "tart" before he ever meets her in person.

Steinbeck, however, counters George's stereotypical condemnation of the woman by undermining the entire scenario of the Garden myth; he intimates that the paradise of the land dream is doomed before Curley's wife ever enters the story. Critics generally agree that the grove in the opening scene, where George and Lennie spend the night before reporting to work at the ranch—the same grove in which George shoots Lennie at the end of the story—symbolizes the dream of owning the farm and "living off the fat of the land." But when Lennie gulps the water from the pool in the grove, George warns him that it might make him sick. "I ain't sure it's good water [George said]. Looks kinda scummy to me." George's comment reveals that, symbolically at least, paradise may already be spoiled. Moreover, later in the play, when George talks about the actual farm that he intends to buy for himself and Lennie, he explains to Candy that he can get the place for a really cheap price, "for six hundred bucks. The ole people that owns it is flat bust." Apparently, the present owners of George's dream farm are not able to live "off the fat of the land," a detail that both he and Candy conveniently overlook. By deliberately bringing this fact to the attention of the audience, Steinbeck creates a tension between George's mythical discourse of the dream life toward which he is striving and the voice of reality, which says that even if George acquired the piece of land that he has in mind, his dream of an Edenic existence would still not be realized.

—Charlotte Cook Hadella, "The Dialogic Tension in Steinbeck's Portrait of Curley's Wife," *John Steinbeck: The Years of Greatness, 1936–1939,* ed. John H. Timmerman (Tuscaloosa: University of Alabama Press, 1993), pp. 68–70

❖

Works by
John Steinbeck

Cup of Gold: A Life of Henry Morgan, Buccaneer, with Occasional Reference to History. 1929.

The Pastures of Heaven. 1932.

To a God Unknown. 1933.

Tortilla Flat. 1935.

In Dubious Battle. 1936.

Saint Katy the Virgin. 1936.

Nothing So Monstrous. 1936.

Of Mice and Men. 1937.

Of Mice and Men (drama; with George S. Kaufman). 1937.

The Red Pony. 1937.

The Long Valley. 1938.

Their Blood Is Strong. 1938.

The Grapes of Wrath. 1939.

John Steinbeck Replies. 1940.

The Forgotten Village. 1941.

Sea of Cortez: A Leisurely Journal of Travel and Research (with Edward F. Ricketts). 1941.

Bombs Away: The Story of a Bomber Team. 1942.

The Moon Is Down. 1942.

The Moon Is Down (drama). 1943.

The Steinbeck Pocket Book. Ed. Pascal Covici. 1943.

How Edith McGillcuddy Met R L S. 1943.

Cannery Row. 1945.

The Portable Steinbeck. Ed. Pascal Covici. 1946.

The Pearl. 1947.

Vanderbilt Clinic. 1947.

The Wayward Bus. 1947.

The First Watch. 1947.

A Russian Journal. 1948.

The Steinbeck Omnibus. 1950.

Burning Bright: A Play in Story Form. 1950.

Burning Bright (drama). 1951.

Viva Zapata! 1951, 1991 (as *Zapata*).

The Log from the Sea of Cortez. 1951.

East of Eden. 1952.

Short Novels. 1953.

Sweet Thursday. 1954.

Positano. 1954.

The Short Reign of Pippin IV: A Fabrication. 1957.

The Chrysanthemums. 1957.

Once There Was a War. 1958.

The Winter of Our Discontent. 1961.

Travels with Charley in Search of America. 1962.

Speech Accepting the Nobel Prize for Literature. c. 1962.

A Letter from John Steinbeck. 1964.

Letters to Alicia. 1965.

America and Americans. 1966.

The Journal of a Novel: The East of Eden Letters. 1969.

John Steinbeck: His Language. 1970.

Steinbeck: A Life in Letters. Ed. Elaine Steinbeck and Robert Wallsten. 1975.

The Acts of King Arthur and His Noble Knights, from the Winchester Manuscripts of Malory and Other Sources. 1976.

The Collected Poems of Amnesia Glasscock. 1976.

Letters to Elizabeth: A Selection of Letters from John Steinbeck to Elizabeth Otis. Ed. Florian J. Shasky and Susan F. Riggs. 1978.

Flight. 1979.

A Letter of Inspiration. 1980.

Selected Essays. Ed. Kiyoshi Nakayama and Hidekazu Hirose. 1981.

Your Only Weapon Is Your Work: A Letter by John Steinbeck to Dennis Murphy. 1985.

Uncollected Stories. Ed. Kiyoshi Nakayama. 1986.

Always Something to Do in Salinas. 1986.

John Steinbeck on Writing. Ed. Tetsumaro Hayashi. 1988.

Working Days: The Journals of The Grapes of Wrath, *1938–1941.* Ed. Robert DeMott. 1989.

"Their Blood Is Strong." 1989.

Breakfast: A Short Story. 1990.

Novels and Stories, 1932–1937. 1994.

Works about John Steinbeck and *Of Mice and Men*

Astro, Richard. *John Steinbeck and Edward F. Ricketts: The Shaping of a Novelist.* Minneapolis: University of Minnesota Press, 1973.

Bellman, Samuel I. "Control and Freedom in Steinbeck's *Of Mice and Men.*" *CEA Critic* 38 (1975): 25–27.

Benson, Jackson J. *The True Adventures of John Steinbeck, Writer: A Biography.* New York: Viking Press, 1983.

Bloom, Harold, ed. *John Steinbeck.* New York: Chelsea House, 1987.

Brown, John Mason. "Mr. John Steinbeck's *Of Mice and Men.*" In Brown's *Two on the Aisle: Ten Years of the American Theatre in Performance.* New York: W. W. Norton, 1938, pp. 183–87.

Cardullo, Robert. "On the Road to Tragedy: The Function of Candy in *Of Mice and Men.*" In *All the World: Drama Past and Present II,* ed. Karelisa V. Hartigan. Washington, DC: University Press of America, 1982, pp. 1–8.

Davac, Lee. "Lennie as Christian in *Of Mice and Men.*" *Southwestern American Literature* 4 (1974): 87–91.

Davison, Richard Allan. "Of Mice and Men and McTeague: Steinbeck, Fitzgerald, and Frank Norris." *Studies in American Fiction* 17 (1989): 219–26.

French, Warren. "John Steinbeck and American Literature." *San Jose Studies* 13, No. 2 (Spring 1987): 35–48.

———. *John Steinbeck's Fiction, Revisited.* New York: Twayne, 1994.

———. *Steinbeck and D. H. Lawrence: Fictive Voices and the Ethical Imperative.* Muncie, IN: John Steinbeck Society of America, 1972.

Gladstein, Mimi Reisel. *The Indestructible Woman in Faulkner, Hemingway, and Steinbeck.* Ann Arbor, MI: UMI Research Press, 1986.

Gray, James. *John Steinbeck.* Minneapolis: University of Minnesota Press, 1971.

Gurko, Leo. "*Of Mice and Men:* Steinbeck as Manichean." *University of Windsor Review* 8 (1973): 11–23.

Hayashi, Tetsumaro, ed. *Steinbeck's Women: Essays in Criticism.* Muncie, IN: John Steinbeck Society of America, 1979.

Hyman, Stanley Edgar. "Some Notes on John Steinbeck." *Antioch Review* 2 (1942): 185–200.

Jones, Lawrence William. *John Steinbeck as Fabulist.* Ed. Marston LaFrance. Muncie, IN: John Steinbeck Society of America, 1973.

Kauffmann, Stanley. "*Of Mice and Men.*" In Kauffmann's *Persons of the Drama.* New York: Harper & Row, 1976, pp. 156–59.

Kiernan, Thomas. *The Intricate Music: A Biography of John Steinbeck.* Boston: Little, Brown, 1979.

Lieber, Todd M. "Talismanic Patterns in the Novels of John Steinbeck." *American Literature* 44 (1972): 262–75.

Lisca, Peter. *John Steinbeck: Nature and Myth.* New York: Crowell, 1978.

———. *The Wide World of John Steinbeck.* New Brunswick, NJ: Rutgers University Press, 1958.

Marks, Lester Jay. *Thematic Design in the Novels of John Steinbeck.* The Hague: Mouton, 1969.

Millichap, Joseph. "Realistic Style in Steinbeck's and Milestone's *Of Mice and Men.*" *Literature/Film Quarterly* 6 (1978): 241–52.

Modern Fiction Studies 11, No. 1 (Spring 1965). Special John Steinbeck issue.

Noble, Donald R., ed. *The Steinbeck Question: New Essays in Criticism.* Troy, NY: Whitston, 1993.

Owen, Louis. *John Steinbeck's Re-Vision of America.* Athens: University of Georgia Press, 1985.

Parini, Jay. *John Steinbeck: A Biography.* London: Heinemann, 1994.

Pratt, John Clark. *John Steinbeck: A Critical Essay.* Grand Rapids, MI: William B. Eerdmans, 1970.

St. Pierre, Brian. *John Steinbeck: The California Years.* San Francisco: Chronicle Books, 1983.

Scheer, Ronald. "*Of Mice and Men:* Novel, Play, Movie." *American Examiner* 6 (1978–79): 6–39.

Shurgot, Michael W. "A Game of Cards in Steinbeck's *Of Mice and Men.*" *Steinbeck Quarterly* 15, Nos. 1/2 (Winter–Spring 1982): 38–43.

Simmonds, Roy S. *Steinbeck's Literary Achievements.* Muncie, IN: John Steinbeck Society of America, 1976.

Spilka, Mark. "Of George and Lennie and Curley's Wife: Sweet Violence in Steinbeck's Eden." *Modern Fiction Studies* 20 (1974): 169–79.

Tedlock, E. W., Jr., and C. V. Wicker, ed. *Steinbeck and His Critics: A Record of Twenty-five Years.* Albuquerque: University of New Mexico Press, 1965.

Waldron, Edward E. "Using Literature to Teach Ethical Principles in Medicine: *Of Mice and Men* and the Concept of Duty." *Literature and Medicine* 7 (1988): 170–76.

Index of
Themes and Ideas